CONTEMPORARY ISSUES

GENDER EQUALITY

CONTEMPORARY ISSUES

CRIMINAL JUSTICE SYSTEM
EDUCATION
THE ENVIRONMENT
GENDER EQUALITY
GUN CONTROL
HEALTH CARE
IMMIGRATION
JOBS AND ECONOMY
MENTAL HEALTH
POVERTY AND WELFARE
PRIVACY AND SOCIAL MEDIA
RACE RELATIONS
RELIGIOUS FREEDOM

CONTEMPORARY ISSUES

GENDER EQUALITY

MARK R. WHITTINGTON

MC

MASON CREST
450 Parkway Drive, Suite D, Broomall, Pennsylvania 19008
(866) MCP-BOOK (toll-free) • www.masoncrest.com

Printed and bound in the United States of America.

CPSIA Compliance Information: Batch #CCRI2019.
For further information, contact Mason Crest at 1-866-MCP-Book.

First printing
1 3 5 7 9 8 6 4 2

ISBN (hardback) 978-1-4222-4391-6
ISBN (series) 978-1-4222-4387-9
ISBN (ebook) 978-1-4222-7406-4

Library of Congress Cataloging-in-Publication Data
on file at the Library of Congress

Interior and cover design: Torque Advertising + Design
Production: Michelle Luke

Publisher's Note: Websites listed in this book were active at the time of publication. The publisher is not responsible for websites that have changed their address or discontinued operation since the date of publication. The publisher reviews and updates the websites each time the book is reprinted.

QR CODES AND LINKS TO THIRD-PARTY CONTENT

You may gain access to certain third-party content ("Third-Party Sites") by scanning and using the QR Codes that appear in this publication (the "QR Codes"). We do not operate or control in any respect any information, products, or services on such Third-Party Sites linked to by us via the QR Codes included in this publication, and we assume no responsibility for any materials you may access using the QR Codes. Your use of the QR Codes may be subject to terms, limitations, or restrictions set forth in the applicable terms of use or otherwise established by the owners of the Third-Party Sites. Our linking to such Third-Party Sites via the QR Codes does not imply an endorsement or sponsorship of such Third-Party Sites or the information, products, or services offered on or through the Third-Party Sites, nor does it imply an endorsement or sponsorship of this publication by the owners of such Third-Party Sites.

CONTENTS

KEY ICONS TO LOOK FOR:

Words to Understand: These words with their easy-to-understand definitions will increase the reader's understanding of the text while building vocabulary skills.

Sidebars: This boxed material within the main text allows readers to build knowledge, gain insights, explore possibilities, and broaden their perspectives by weaving together additional information to provide realistic and holistic perspectives.

Educational videos: Readers can view videos by scanning our QR codes, providing them with additional educational content to supplement the text. Examples include news coverage, moments in history, speeches, iconic sports moments, and much more!

Text-Dependent Questions: These questions send the reader back to the text for more careful attention to the evidence presented there.

Research Projects: Readers are pointed toward areas of further inquiry connected to each chapter. Suggestions are provided for projects that encourage deeper research and analysis.

Series Glossary of Key Terms: This back-of-the-book glossary contains terminology used throughout this series. Words found here increase the reader's ability to read and comprehend higher-level books and articles in this field.

WORDS TO UNDERSTAND

feminism—the belief that women should have legal rights and social consideration that are equal to men.

gender equality—gender equality is achieved when women and men enjoy the same rights and opportunities across all sectors of society, including economic participation and decision-making, and when the different behaviors, aspirations and needs of women and men are equally valued and favored.

reproductive rights—the right of women to control when, how, and even if they will bear children.

CHAPTER 1

GENDER EQUALITY IN THE UNITED STATES

During the British colonial period of the seventeenth and eighteenth centuries, the colonial governments in North America based their laws on the English common law. This was summarized in Blackstone's Commentaries, which said, "By marriage, the husband and wife are one person in the law. The very being and legal existence of the woman is suspended during the marriage, or at least is incorporated into that of her husband, under whose wing and protection she performs everything."[1]

The concept that women had no separate identity under the law was carried over after the American Revolution. It was assumed that in a family unit, the husband knew what would be best for his family in legal and political matters, which included wives as well as children. The ascent upwards from this state of affairs has been a long and arduous one.

Understandably, many women chafed at this position from the very beginning. Abigail Adams expressed these feelings in a letter to her husband, John Adams, a delegate to the Second Continental Congress in 1776:

> ...and by the way in the new Code of Laws which I suppose it will be necessary for you to make I desire you would remember the ladies, and be more generous and favorable to them than your ancestors. Do not put such unlimited power into the hands of the Husbands. Remember all Men would be tyrants if they could. If particular care and attention is not paid to the Ladies we are determined to foment a Rebellion, and will not hold ourselves bound by any Laws in which we have no voice, or Representation.[2]

What John Adams had to say about his wife's plea for women's rights is lost to history. While he helped to draft the Declaration of Independence, that document and others of early America have little to say about the rights of women. According to Dr. Graham Warder of Keene State College, the status of American women would not begin to change until the nineteenth century:

> In colonial America, men were considered superior to women—in all ways, even in terms of morality. In a world of strict patriarchal hierarchy, men controlled not only wealth and political power but also how their children were raised, religious questions, and all matters of right and wrong. In the early part of the nineteenth century, however, many Americans experienced a revolution in gender. What we now view as old-fashioned and even oppressive was then new and potentially liberating.[3]

Life in America in the nineteenth century for most women was hard. They often had to perform hard labor on rural farms, and that required women to be health and strong. Unfortunately, women often became exhausted, mentally and physically, by the long days of labor. Middle-

and upper-class women had an easier time, because they could afford servants, or in the pre-Civil War south, slaves. The hard labor of managing the household was shared. But with few exceptions, American women were consigned to the traditional role: keeping the hearth and home.

The development of labor-saving devices, both on the farm and in the home, relieved the daily drudgery of women's lives. Industrialization brought job opportunities for urban women outside the home. More women went to school, even to college, though the latter concentrated

Education beyond basic reading and writing was relatively rare for women who lived on the frontier. For those who did go on to attend a high school, often the only career available to women was as a teacher, until they were married and had a family.

on new techniques for home management for the most part. More women could be found in non-traditional roles, such as Nellie Bly, who became a journalist, or Elizabeth Blackwell, the first American woman to graduate from medical school.

The nineteenth century also saw the entry of women into social and political movements. The drive to abolish slavery included many women, some of whom held leadership positions. The Temperance Movement, designed to alleviate the effect of alcoholism on families, was similarly driven by women. Women who became involved in these movements began to see firsthand how they could become involved in political causes far beyond their traditional homemaking sphere. By the late nineteenth century, these woman became activists for suffrage and other social causes. "The end of the nineteenth century was a time of tumult and change, and tensions showed in the lives of women," notes Dr. Warder. "New opportunities in education, employment and social protest caused many women to question the role society cast for them. Involvement in any of these activities often led to unanticipated results and actions that defined new roles for women in the decades that followed."[4]

THE WOMEN'S RIGHTS MOVEMENT

In 1848, Elizabeth Cady Stanton and Lucretia Mott invited a group of abolitionists to meet in Seneca Falls, New York, and discuss the issue of women's rights. Stanton and Mott had been inspired by the World Anti-Slavery Convention in London, where they had meet in 1840. They had been working to end slavery and to gain equal rights for free blacks. Now they wanted to do the same for women.

Both men and women participated in the Women's Rights Convention at Seneca Falls. The delegates there agreed that American women were autonomous individuals and deserved the right to participate fully in politics and the workplace. The delegates produced a document called the Declaration of Sentiments, which proclaimed, "We hold these truths to be self-evident, that all men and women are created equal, that they are endowed by their creator with certain inalienable rights, that among these are life, liberty, and the pursuit of happiness."[5]

The fight for female suffrage lasted many decades reverses and changes in strategy. The campaign featured

To learn more about the women's suffrage movement, scan here.

During the nineteenth century, women like Susan B. Anthony (1820-1906), Lucretia Mott (1793-1880), and Elizabeth Cady Stanton (1815-1902) organized the women's rights movement, seeking the right to vote and engage in politics.

not only peaceful political activism but acts of civil disobedience and even hunger strikes. Western territories admitted as states were among the first to allow women to vote in state and local elections. Finally, on August 26, 1920, the Nineteenth Amendment to the Constitution was ratified, guaranteeing all women the right to vote in elections.

Having gotten the vote and the right to run for office, women spent many decades accumulating political power. Early female political pioneers include Gov. Miriam "Ma" Ferguson, D-Texas and Sen. Margaret Chase Smith, R-Maine. Current female politicians come from the length and breadth of the political spectrum and include Hillary Clinton, Kamala Harris, Nancy Pelosi, and Nikki Haley. Women have held every elected political office except the presidency and vice presidency. And most people believe that will come too, given time and circumstance.

US Senator Kamala Harris, a Democrat from California, campaigns for the party's presidential nomination in New Hampshire, April 2019.

REPRODUCTIVE RIGHTS

While the fight for women's suffrage was reaching its climax, another front for **gender equality** opened, the campaign for **reproductive rights** for women. Margaret Sanger was at the forefront of this fight. Sanger worked as a nurse in New York City's Lower East Side, where many poor immigrants lived. Through her work, Sanger treated a number of women who had undergone back-alley abortions or tried to self-terminate their pregnancies. Sanger wanted to make birth control information and contraceptives available to poor women, so they could control the size of their families. In 1912, Sanger began writing a newspaper column called "What Every Girl Should Know," to educate women about sex. She once declared, "No woman can call herself free until she can choose consciously whether she will or will not be a mother."[6]

The idea that women could control whether they had children was considered outrageous and controversial at the time. At one point, Sanger was obliged to flee to England to avoid a jail sentence for violating the Comstock Act. This law prohibited the sale of "obscene materials," which at the time included information on sex, reproduction, and birth control devices.

Sanger's legal battles resulted in court rulings that relaxed the laws prohibiting birth control. She later founded the precursor of Planned Parenthood and supported research that led to the development of oral contraceptives in the early 1960s.

Sanger's legacy is not without controversy. She was a believer in a concept called "eugenics" and advocated birth control as a means to weed out the physically and mentally unfit. She has also been accused by modern conservatives of harboring racist views, believing that birth control could be used to reduce the population of African Americans and other ethnic groups. The accusation is hotly disputed by Sanger's admirers.

Another controversy rising out of the fight for reproductive rights was the establishment of legal abortion

Women hold up signs in front of the US Supreme Court building in Washington, DC, to protest state laws that would restrict abortion rights.

resulting from the landmark Supreme Court *Roe v. Wade* ruling in 1973. The ruling has sparked a grinding, emotion-filled fight between the concept that legal abortion is crucial for women's health and reproductive choice and the belief by many that an embryo is a human life from the moment of conception. While many Americans are in the middle of the controversy, supporting legal abortion with some restrictions, the matter has been defined by the two extremes since the *Roe v. Wade* case. The two sides are not reconcilable.

THE FEMINIST MOVEMENT

The women's rights movement in the United States, sometimes called **feminism**, can be broken into several different periods, or waves. The "first wave" of feminism occurred during the nineteenth and early twentieth centuries, and focused on gaining legal rights for women, especially the right to vote. The "second wave" of feminism occurred during the 1960s and 1970s, and touched on every area of women's experience: politics, work, the family, and sexuality. It is sometimes known by the name "women's liberation movement."

Spurred on by the writings of Simone de Beauvoir, Betty Friedan, and Gloria Steinem, the feminist movement of the 1960s and 1970s won important court and legislative victories for women. The 1963 Equal Pay Act promised equal pay for equal work regardless of several characteristics, including gender. Supreme Court rulings such as *Griswold v. Connecticut* and *Eisenstadt v. Baird* removed the final laws that restricted womens' access to contraceptives. An organization called the National Organization for Women (NOW) was created, touting itself as the women's version of the NAACP.

In 1972, the Equal Employment Opportunity Act gave the EEOC the authority to file lawsuits against employers

Suffragists demonstrate on the steps of the US Capitol building, May 1914. The suffragists were women who fought for the right to vote in American elections. Their activities led to ratification of the Nineteenth Amendment to the US Constitution in August 1920.

With banners demanding equality, women march through Washington, D.C., in 1970.

that discriminated against women. This law helped stop workplace discrimination. Another law, the Equal Credit Opportunity Act of 1974, prohibited discrimination based on sex or marital status. This meant a married woman could walk into a bank and open an account in her name. She could sign up for a credit card in her own name. Or she could take out a loan. Before then, banks were allowed to require a husband's signature before they would extend credit, or a woman's credit card could be canceled if she got divorced.

Other changes included the liberalization of divorce laws, as well as the legalization of abortion thanks to the

> ***"A gender-equal society would be one where the word 'gender' does not exist: where everyone can be themselves."[7]***
>
> ***—Gloria Steinem, Feminist writer and political activist***

1973 Supreme Court ruling in *Roe v. Wade*. In 1972 Congress passed Title IX of the Higher Education Act, which prohibited discrimination based on sex in any educational program receiving federal funds. This forced all-male schools to open their doors to women, and schools to create athletic teams for women. And record numbers of women ran for—and started winning—political office.

A major goal of the feminist movement was to pass an Equal Rights Amendment (ERA) to the United States Constitution. The Equal Rights Amendment had been written by a small group of authors, led by Alice Paul,

"Society as a whole benefits immeasurably from a climate in which all persons, regardless of race or gender, may have the opportunity to earn respect, responsibility, advancement, and remuneration based on ability."[8]

—Sandra Day O'Connor, the first woman appointed to the US Supreme Court

in 1923. It had been introduced in every Congressional session after that, but was either voted down or never voted upon. The text of the ERA was simple:

> Section 1. Equality of Rights under the law shall not be denied or abridged by the United States or any state on account of sex.
>
> Section 2. The Congress shall have the power to enforce, by appropriate legislation, the provisions of this article.
>
> Section 3. This amendment shall take effect two years after the date of ratification.[9]

The ERA finally passed Congress in 1972. All that was left was for the ERA to be ratified by the 38 of the 50 state legislatures, and it would become a federal law. At first, the ratifications came quickly. Thirty states ratified the amendment by the end of 1973. It seemed like the amendment would become law long before a seven-year deadline expired in March 1979.

But then a backlash against the amendment started. Ironically, the opposition was led by a woman named

Alice Paul (1885–1977), founder of the National Woman's Party, raises a glass to celebrate ratification of the Nineteenth Amendment, 1920. Her organization had been instrumental in getting the amendment passed into law. Over the next five decades, Paul worked toward ratification of an Equal Rights Amendment to the Constitution.

Phyllis Schlafly. She was a conservative who regarded the ERA and the feminist movement as an assault on the family and traditional values. The pace of ratification suddenly dropped off. Three states ratified the ERA during 1974, one in 1975, none in 1976, and one in 1977.

With progress on ratification stalled, Congress in 1978 passed a controversial extension of the deadline, bringing

Phyllis Schlafly, wearing a "Stop ERA" badge, demonstrates with other women against the Equal Rights Amendment in front of the White House, 1977.

it to June 30, 1982. Despite the additional thirty-nine months, no more states ratified the amendment. The extended deadline came and went with the Equal Rights Amendment three states short of becoming federal law. It was a bitter defeat for feminists.

"The failure of the ERA was followed in the 1980s by a gradual decline in organized, often bellicose activity by masses of women in the United States," notes an *Encyclopedia Britannica* essay. "Moreover, there was a growing national sense that the core goals of the women's rights movement had been achieved."[10]

FEMINISM TODAY

The "third wave" of the feminist movement is generally said to have begun in the early 1990s, and continues today. Third-wave feminism embraces more diversity than did the previous waves. Many women who identify with the third wave say they are seeking individual empowerment. They are less concerned with being part of a unified movement.

The third wave of feminism has been driven largely by women who were born since the 1970s. These younger women benefited from the gains secured by second-wave feminists. They grew up enjoying a higher degree of equality with males. They had more educational and professional opportunities than their mothers did.

Many women who identify with the third wave say that feminism should be about justice for everyone. They believe feminists should be at the forefront of the fight against all forms of discrimination. In their view, racism or prejudice against gays is just as unacceptable as sexism. And, they say, all forms of oppression arise from similar impulses. Third-wave feminists also tend to take a global outlook, hoping to improve the lives of women all over the world, not just in the United States.

Today, many women actively protest against social injustices. However, their activities are more likely to be directed toward improving society for everyone, rather than being focused solely on gender issues.

TEXT-DEPENDENT QUESTIONS

1. What did Abigail Adams ask her husband while he was participating in the Second Continental Congress in 1776?
2. Which two social movements in nineteenth-century America contributed leaders and workers to the suffrage campaign?
3. What was the purpose of the Equal Rights Amendment?

RESEARCH PROJECTS

Write an essay detailing some instance when you feel you were discriminated against because of your gender. The discrimination could be legal, social, or even political, based solely on your gender and perceptions derived thereby. The act of discrimination could range from not being admitted to a university to other people making unfair assumptions based on your gender.

WORDS TO UNDERSTAND

gender wage gap—the difference between what men and women are paid.

pay equity legislation—laws that require companies to provide equal pay for men and women who are doing the same work.

wage discrimination—a policy, explicit or implicit, that compensates women less than men for work of equal value.

CHAPTER 2

CAN THE WAGE GAP BE CLOSED THROUGH LEGISLATION?

Women make up almost half of the workforce. In most American families with children, they are either the sole breadwinner or contribute to the family's income through their work. Each year, women earn more college and graduate degrees than men. Yet, on average, women continue to earn less than men for their work. Today, data indicates that full-time, year-round female workers earn about 80 cents for every dollar that a male worker earns. This is a **gender wage gap** of 20 percent.

The gender pay gap occurs across almost all occupations and industries. Male-dominated industries such as trucking, carpentry, construction, and automotive services tend to have higher wages than industries and occupations made up mostly of female workers, such as nursing, social work, counseling, and human resources. The wage gap is even broader for African-American and Hispanic women, and factors like motherhood or single-parent status also have a depressing effect on womens' wages.

In some occupations, women collectively receive billions less than men. For instance, a report by the American Association of University Women found that

LILLY LEDBETTER'S STORY

Title VII of the Civil Rights Act of 1964 made it illegal for businesses to discriminate against women or minorities in employment. But the passage of that landmark law didn't completely end discrimination. Some businesses managed to hide their unfair practices. That was a lesson Lilly Ledbetter learned.

Ledbetter, who was born in 1938, went to work at the Goodyear Tire and Rubber plant in Gadsden, Alabama, in 1979. She was an overnight supervisor at the plant for almost twenty years. Ledbetter got good job reviews. In 1996, she was honored with Goodyear's Top Performance Award.

Two years later, as she was about to retire, someone at the Goodyear plant told Ledbetter she was making less money than men who did the same job. Ledbetter investigated, and soon found out that she'd been receiving less than her male colleagues for a long time.

Ledbetter filed a complaint. Soon afterward, her bosses assigned the sixty-year-old supervisor to lift heavy tires at the plant. She believed this was to get back at her for the complaint. Soon she filed a lawsuit.

women who work as doctors or surgeons are paid $19 billion less annually than if they were paid the same as men in that occupation.

"Women, on average, earn less than men in nearly every single occupation for which there is sufficient earnings data for both men and women to calculate an

It charged that Goodyear had unlawfully underpaid her $60,000 over the course of her career.

Ledbetter won the lawsuit. A jury awarded her $3.3 million, but a judge later reduced the amount to about $300,000. However, Goodyear appealed the decision. The case ended up before the Supreme Court.

In 2007, the Court voted 5–4 that Ledbetter wasn't entitled to receive any damages from Goodyear. The reason? The justices said that Title VII required people to bring a claim of pay discrimination within 180 days of the first instance of such discrimination.

Many people found the Supreme Court's decision hard to accept. Ledbetter hadn't known about her unfair treatment until many years after it began. How could she have filed a complaint in the time allowed?

Lawmakers decided to address the situation. In January 2009, Congress passed, and President Barack Obama signed, the Lilly Ledbetter Fair Pay Act. The law allows workers to file a complaint 180 days from the last instance of pay discrimination they believe they've suffered.

earnings ratio," notes a 2018 report titled "Pay Equity and Discrimination" by the Institute for Women's Policy Research. "In middle-skill occupations, workers in jobs mainly done by women earn only 66 percent of workers in jobs mainly done by men. IWPR's report on sex and race discrimination in the workplace shows that outright discrimination in pay, hiring, or promotions continues to be a significant feature of working life."[11]

One proposal to close the gender wage gap is the Paycheck Fairness Act, a proposed law that is being considered by the US Congress. The law would amend the Fair Labor Standards Act of 1938 (FLSA) to make employers who violate sex discrimination prohibitions liable for either compensatory or punitive damages through lawsuits.

To watch a news report on the wage gap, scan here.

Activists, community leaders, union members, and politicians gather on the steps of City Hall in New York to rally against gender pay disparity on "Equal Pay Day," April 2, 2019.

It would also provide funding for programs to help female workers gain skills to negotiate fair salaries. The act also directs the US Secretary of Labor to conduct studies and provide information to employers, labor organizations, and the general public regarding the various ways to eliminate the pay disparity between men and women.

The Paycheck Fairness Act has been introduced in every session of Congress since 1997. The bill was approved by the US House of Representatives in 2009, though final approval of the legislation was blocked by Republicans in the US Senate before the legislative session ended. In March 2019, the House of Representatives again passed the Paycheck Fairness Act, although once again it seemed unlikely to pass in the Republican-controlled Senate.

Why is the bill so hard to pass? And should it pass as a remedy for the gender pay gap? The essays on the follow pages examine some of the arguments for and against attempting to pass federal legislation that would close the gender wage gap.

Protesters at a 2017 women's march in Washington, D.C.

LEGISLATION CAN HELP TO CLOSE THE GENDER PAY GAP

More than fifty years ago, the Equal Pay Act of 1963 (EPA) made it illegal for employers to pay unequal wages to men and women in the same workplace who perform substantially equal work. Despite this, gender-based **wage discrimination** remains a problem in the workplace.

This wage gap cannot be dismissed as the inevitable by-product of women's choices in education, career, and family matters. There have been many studies over the past two decades that show that even when all relevant career and family factors are considered, an unexplained gap between men's and women's earnings remains.

For example, an analysis published in 2015 by the US Bureau of Labor Statistics found that women earn less than men who perform substantially the same jobs in the twenty most common occupations for women and in all but one of the twenty most common occupations for men.

Another study, undertaken by the American Association of University Women, found that the pay gap between female and male college graduates cannot fully be accounted for by factors known to affect wages, such as experience (including work hours), training, education, and personal characteristics. "A portion of the pay gap that remains unexplained after all other factors are taken into account is five percent one year after graduation and 12 percent 10 years after graduation," concluded the report. "These unexplained gaps are evidence of discrimination,

> *"I do not demand equal pay for any women save those who do equal work in value. Scorn to be coddled by your employers; make them understand that you are in their service as workers, not as women."*[12]
>
> *—Susan B. Anthony, women's rights activist*

which remains a serious problem for women in the work force.'"[13]

As the American Association of University Women notes, state laws have proven inadequate to close the gender pay gap across the nation. Although more than half of the states have **pay equity legislation**, the gender wage gap remains. Laws at the federal level, such as the Paycheck Fairness Act, are still required to make sure that all Americans benefit from the same policies and protections.

Among the state laws that do seem to be most effective are ones that prevent employers from asking job applicants how much they earned in a previous job. The purpose of these laws is to break the cycle of pay disparity by removing the link between past inequalities and salary negotiations. California and Massachusetts already have these restrictions in place, and so does New York City and

President Barack Obama signs executive orders to strengthen the enforcement of equal pay laws for women in April 2014. Lilly Ledbetter stands to the left of the signing table.

the territory of Puerto Rico. Similar measures are under consideration in more than a dozen other states.

Increasing transparency in salaries would also help address the gender wage gap. Many people find talking about money to be awkward, and companies often discourage people from discussing their salaries with their co-workers. However, the secrecy around pay helps to perpetuate inequality.

A 2018 study conducted by the *Harvard Business Review* found that when laws require companies to disclose gender pay disparities, the gender wage gap shrinks and more women are hired and promoted to senior roles. However, the study also notes that wages become more equal because men in such cases tend to be paid less, rather than women earning more.

The National Organization for Women (NOW) notes that progress has been steady but much too slow under current legislation. "The progress of women in the workforce over the last fifty-six years is evident, but the financial penalty many women experience due to sex- and race-based pay discrimination must stop," notes a NOW statement. "If closing the wage gap continues at its agonizingly slow current rate, men and women will not reach wage equality until 2059. That is forty years too long."[14]

Greater salary transparency would help women to negotiate fair wages, as they could see what other similarly qualified candidates are earning in the same position.

LEGISLATION WOULD NOT SOLVE THE WAGE GAP AND WOULD UNFAIRLY INHIBIT BUSINESSES

Researchers have identified many reasons why most of the gender wage gap results from the different choices women and men make in the workplace, rather than a result of systematic discrimination.

One factor in the different pay amounts is that a higher percentage of women are employed part-time. More men work full-time, and full-time employment tends to pay more than part-time work.

Another factor is that women are more likely to leave the labor force to have children, raise families, and take care of elders. While they may re-enter the workforce, some of the wage gap can be explained by the percentage of women who leave the labor force each year for these reasons.

Women, especially working mothers, also tend to value "family friendly" workplace policies more than men. This affects the jobs that they take and the places where the work, and may inhibit their earnings.

Research from the Bureau of Labor Statistics also indicates that women are more likely to value non-wage benefits—health insurance and other fringe benefits—more than men do. As a result, these make up a greater portion of their compensation—yet are not necessarily counted in studies that compare male and female wages.

"Although additional research in this area is clearly needed, this study leads to the unambiguous conclusion that the differences in the compensation of men and women are the result of a multitude of factors and that the raw wage gap should not be used as the basis to justify corrective action," notes an analysis by CONSAD Research Corporation. "Indeed, there may be nothing to correct. The differences in raw wages may be almost entirely the result of the individual choices being made by both male and female workers."[15]

Christina Hoff Sommers, a scholar at the American Enterprise Institute, points out that equality is not necessarily the same thing as fairness. She has noted some

"Why can't there be an acknowledgment that, in some instances, women remove themselves from the workforce for a long time, and when they come back, of course they're not going to get exactly equal pay?"[16]

—Megyn Kelly, American TV commentator

potential problems with the Paycheck Fairness Act. "Under the bill, it's not enough for an employer to guard against intentional discrimination; it also has to police potentially discriminatory assumptions behind market-driven wage disparities that have nothing to do with sexism," writes Sommers:

> Universities, for example, typically pay professors in their business schools more than they pay those in the school of social work, citing market forces as the justification. But according to the gender theory that informs this bill, sexist attitudes led society to place a higher value on male-centered fields like business than on female-centered fields like social work.
>
> The bill's language regarding these 'lingering effects' is vague, but that's the problem: it could prove a legal nightmare for even the best-intentioned employers. The theory will be elaborated in feminist expert testimony when cases go to trial, and it's not hard to imagine a media firestorm developing from it. Faced with multimillion-dollar lawsuits and the attendant publicity, many innocent employers would choose to settle.[17]

Citing a study by Allan Dinkoff for the employment law firm Weil, Gotshal & Manges, Daniel Fisher found that the Paycheck Fairness Bill would impose undue burdens on business in terms of compensation. Fisher explains that under the current laws, companies have the flexibility to respond to a new hire's salary history or their compensation demands. He provides the example of a company that hires a male and female shipping clerk ("John" and "Sally"), offering both a salary of $30,000. If the male clerk insists that he wants to be paid $33,000, and the company decides it is in their interest to agree to this salary figure, they are not liable under the current

Pay discrimination already is illegal, so new legislation like the Paycheck Fairness Act will only result in creating rigid pay scales that limit the flexibility of businesses to hire productive workers.

PATERNITY LEAVE

One of the reasons cited for the gender pay gap is that women, rather than men, tend to take maternity leave when their children are born. The Family and Medical Leave Act of 1993 requires companies of more than fifty people to allow both parents of a new child to take leave, though it does not require that such leave be paid.

Studies indicate that fathers who take off work when their children are born tend to be more involved in their care, and there are many other benefits to their families as well. So why don't more men take, what is in effect, paternity leave? The answer resides in workplace culture.

"Our workplace culture, and the male breadwinner norm, is a barrier for men seeking to take more extended paternity leaves," writes Patty Hilger. "Even where men have access to paid leave, they might still cut their leaves short to avoid being perceived as less dedicated employees.

"In addition ... many fathers face the harsh (tangible) reality that they simply cannot afford to take unpaid time off, especially if the mother of the child is also taking unpaid time off. With unpaid family leave as the standard, fathers generally get the least opportunity to take time off."[18]

law because the worker's gender was not the reason he was paid more. "The result would be very different under the Paycheck Fairness Act, which eliminates the 'reason other than sex' defense and substitutes instead a requirement that the employer prove that its pay practices are divorced from any discrimination in its workplace or at the employee's prior workplace, that the pay practice is job related, and that it is consistent with 'business necessity,'" writes Fisher.

Men who take time off work for family obligations could experience long-term negative effects on their career, like lower pay or being passed over for promotions.

“So, now employers must have one pay for a job, not only at the entry level, but throughout the organization. ... Therefore, companies will have far less flexibility in addressing different salary histories for new hires, different salary demands from existing employees, the size of pay raises for people promoted into new roles, and so on. The law would make these changes without real evidence that these steps will eliminate pay disparities between men and women or any thought on the impact of restricting a company’s ability to respond to the different needs and demands of its employees.”[19]

In short, federal laws like the Paycheck Fairness Act would do little to close the gender wage gap, because of the other factors that create this gap. Instead, such laws would create unforeseen and unfair burdens for businesses, which could hurt the very workers that the law purports to help.

TEXT-DEPENDENT QUESTIONS

1. How much do working women earn for each dollar that a man earns today?
2. In what year will men and women reach pay equity under current law, according to the National Organization for Women?
3. What are some factors other than systematic discrimination that could explain the gender wage gap?

RESEARCH PROJECTS

Have the class write essays describing what they value in a future job they might apply for as adults. Do they want high salaries or do they favor more family friendly practices? Have the teacher analyze the essays and see if there is a difference between male and female students. Then hold a classroom discussion.

WORDS TO UNDERSTAND

litigant—a person who is involved in a lawsuit.

rape—forced sexual intercourse, including vaginal, anal, or oral penetration. Penetration may be by a body part or an object.

sexual assault—any type of sexual contact or behavior that occurs without the explicit consent of the recipient, including rape.

sexual harassment—behavior that includes unwelcome sexual advances, requests for sexual favors, and other verbal or physical harassment of a sexual nature.

CHAPTER 3

HAS THE #METOO MOVEMENT GONE TOO FAR?

For most of American history, women in the workplace silently endured mistreatment, with few protections available. During the eighteenth and nineteenth centuries, black female slaves in the South were often **raped** or forced into sexual encounters with their white masters. This was also true of domestic servants, both white and black, who lived and worked in the northern states. During the early twentieth century, as growing numbers of women began to find employment in garment shops and other factories, or in clerical positions, often faced verbal taunts and unwanted sexual advances from their male supervisors.

"For decades, there were few significant changes in the ways women were treated at work," writes Sascha Cohen in *Time*. "Those who complained discovered that sexually predatory behavior on the job was dismissed as trivial and harmless. Women rarely talked openly about the issue, although the situation only became more pressing as their participation in the workforce increased throughout the 1960s and 1970s."[20]

Things started to slowly turn around in the 1970s, as the modern feminist movement began to challenge the cultural standards that failed to recognize women's right to consent. At meetings, women shared their stories about harassment in the workplace and realized that they were not alone in their experiences.

In 1975, a woman named Carmita Wood filed a claim for unemployment benefits after she resigned from her job at Cornell University due to unwanted touching from her supervisor. "Cornell had refused Wood's request for a transfer, and denied her the benefits on the grounds that she quit for 'personal reasons,'" writes Cohen. "Wood together with activists at the university's Human Affairs Office, formed a group called Working Women United. At a Speak Out event hosted by the group, secretaries, mailroom clerks, filmmakers, factory workers, and waitresses shared their stories, revealing that the problem

To hear young people's stories about the #MeToo Movement, scan here.

extended beyond the university setting. The women spoke of masturbatory displays, threats and pressure to trade sexual favors for promotions."[21] It was during this case that the phrase **sexual harassment** was created.

"By 1977, three court cases confirmed that a woman could sue her employer for harassment under Title VII of the 1964 Civil Rights Act, using the EEOC as the vehicle for redress. The Supreme Court upheld these early cases in 1986 with *Meritor Savings Bank v. Vinson*, which was based

Unwanted sexual advances, and verbal or physical conduct of a sexual nature, can create an intimidating, hostile, or offensive work environment.

on the complaints of Mechelle Vinson, a bank employee whose boss intimidated her into having sex with him in vaults and basements up to fifty times. Vinson was African American, as were many of the **litigants** in pioneering sexual harassment cases; some historians suggest that the success of racial discrimination cases during these same

WHEN MEN ARE SEXUALLY HARASSED

Civil case law does not distinguish between genders where it comes to sexual harassment. Women can sexually harass men. Indeed, men can sexually harass men. How prevalent is the sexual harassment of men? It's more common than most people think. In a recent survey, reported in *Psychology Today*, about one-third of all working men reported experiencing at least one form of sexual harassment in the previous year. More than one out of every six sexual harassment charges filed US Equal Employment Opportunity Commission (EEOC) each year are filed by men.

"Despite the serious consequences that can stem from sexual harassment, whether it involves men or women, sexual harassment against men is often not taken that seriously," notes psychologist Romeo Vitalli. "There has been extensive research looking at how sexual harassment can affect women, both in

years encouraged women of color to vigorously pursue their rights at work."[22]

The 1991 Supreme Court confirmation hearings of Clarence Thomas brought the issue of sexual harassment into public consciousness. During the hearings a woman named Anita Hill testified that when she worked with Thomas in the US Department of Education, and later at the EEOC, he had subjected her to crude, sexually explicit language.

The hearings became extremely contentious, with

terms of the emotional consequences and reduced job prospects, but fewer studies have looked at how men are affected."[23]

Vitalli found that sexual harassment of men ranges from offensive jokes to outright demands for sexual favors in return for career advancement. Gay men, or those that challenge traditional gender rolls, are more likely to experience harassment.

The effects of sexual harassment on men are similar to the effects on women. "Not surprisingly, sexual harassment, whether in the form of verbal or physical abuse, had a negative effect on job satisfaction and psychological well-being," writes Vitalli. "Still, being active in feminist causes can also help protect against the negative effects of this kind of harassment, since it can make men feel empowered about their basic rights."[24]

Professor Anita Hill testifies before Congress during Clarence Thomas's confirmation hearings for the US Supreme Court, October 11, 1991.

Thomas's supporters convinced that Hill's accusations were a ploy to prevent the appointment of a black conservative to the Supreme Court. Ultimately, the US Senate confirmed Thomas for a place on the Court by a vote of 52 to 48. But the Anita Hill accusations brought the issue of sexual harassment in the workplace to the forefront of discussion in America.

Since the early 1990s, most businesses have created policies designed to tamp down on sexual harassment. It has also become accepted that sexual harassment does not just include men preying on women. It can be perpetrated by female bosses against male subordinates, as well as along same sex lines.

Despite this, sexual harassment remains a problem. In the fall of 2017, the *New York Times* and the *New Yorker* reported that more than a dozen women had accused powerful movie producer Harvey Weinstein of sexually harassing or raping them. Although Weinstein claimed that any sexual encounters had been consensual, many other women in the film industry soon came forward to report their own experiences. Actress Alyssa Milano tweeted the phrase #MeToo as the Weinstein stories were breaking, and soon it became a national phenomenon, with hundreds of thousands of women tweeting or telling their own stories of abuse.

The #MeToo Movement would soon call out other serial abusers for a variety of misbehavior, including TV

Disgraced movie producer Harvey Weinstein leaves a New York court after being arrested and charged with rape and criminal sex acts in 2018.

journalist Matt Lauer, actor Kevin Spacey, movie director Brett Ratner, comedian Louis C.K., and US Senator Al Franken of Minnesota.

The Movement reached a fever pitch in 2018, when President Donald Trump appointed Brett Kavanaugh to fill a seat on the Supreme Court. After a four-day confirmation hearing before the US Senate Judiciary Committee, news broke that a psychology professor named Christine Blasey Ford had accused Kavanaugh of attempting to **sexually assault** her at a party when they were in high school more than thirty-five years earlier. An additional day of testimony was held. Ford gave compelling testimony, but was vague on details such as when and where the incident took place. Kavanaugh angrily denounced the accusation as a false partisan smear intended to keep him off the Court. Ultimately, Kavanaugh was confirmed by a 50–48 vote.

Some people believe that woman who accuse men of sexual misdeeds should be automatically believed. They note that women rarely make false reports, and in fact often don't report sexual harassment because they fear the consequences or believe that nothing will happen to the other person involved. However, during the Kavanaugh hearings a backlash arose because even some women were concerned that their husbands or sons would not receive the presumption of innocence should they be accused of such behavior. The essays that follow will examine arguments on both sides of this issue.

THE #METOO MOVEMENT HAS GONE TOO FAR, AND MEN ARE VICTIMIZED BY FALSE ACCUSATIONS

The #MeToo movement, popularized after film producer Harvey Weinstein's decades-long abuse of women was revealed in the media in the fall of 2017, has served as a needed disinfectant to expose and sanction powerful men who have used their positions to sexually harass and abuse women. However, the movement has had some decidedly unpleasant effects that suggest that it has gone too far.

A recent article in *Forbes* suggests that men in the workplace have started to be afraid of their female co-workers and are hesitant to work alone with them or mentor them. "A Pew Research Center survey asked respondents whether they thought that the recent focus on sexual harassment had made it harder for men to know how to interact with women in the workplace. Fifty-one percent of all adults questioned said yes," noted the *Forbes* article:

> Lean In [a non-profit organization formed to help working women] partnered with SurveyMonkey to look into the possible negative effects of the #MeToo movement for women's advancement. Promoting mentorship is one of Lean In's key priorities. Nearly half of male managers they surveyed reported being 'uncomfortable participating in a common work activity with a woman, such as mentoring, working alone, or socializing together.' Senior men were five times more likely to hesitate to travel for work with a junior level woman than with a junior level man."[25]

The article suggests that false accusations of sexual harassment are very rare. However, those fears do

> *"Non-consensual, sexual advances are not the same as flirtatious comments from a creepy dude. The degree of harassment matters."*[26]
>
> *—Cheryl Yeoh, entrepreneur and public speaker*

exist, because merely being accused of inappropriate behavior carries a stigma that could be career killing. Admonishments that men should just learn to behave themselves are inadequate to address this potential problem.

Another way that #MeToo has spiraled out of control is that it has expanded beyond its original purpose of exposing sexual harassment. Tarana Burke, an activist who originally coined the phrase #MeToo in 2006, more than a decade before the Weinstein revelations, told *The*

Women gather in Santa Monica, California, to protest against Brett Kavanaugh's nomination as an associate justice of the US Supreme Court in September 2018.

Atlantic that she fears that the new movement is trying to include and address all sorts of women's issues. "Part of the challenge that we have right now," Burke said, "is everybody trying to couch everything under #MeToo.'"[27]

A political movement that is about everything can lose momentum due to lack of focus and disagreements over which issues are more important.

Finally, an Ipsos Poll suggests that the issue of sexual harassment has become a partisan political issue:

> For example, 80 percent of men and 73 percent of women believe that those who are accused of sexual harassment should be given the benefit of the doubt until proven otherwise—a seven-point difference. Not only is the partisan gap much larger at sixteen percentage points (70 percent of Democrats vs. 86 percent of Republicans), it has widened since our initial study on sexual harassment conducted last year (75 percent of Democrats vs. 80 percent of Republicans, a five-point difference). In another example, there is a seventeen-point difference between Democrats and Republicans that agree it is sometimes difficult to tell what constitutes sexual assault (56 percent of Republicans vs. 39 percent of Democrats), and a twenty-six-point difference when the same question is asked about sexual harassment (65 percent of Republicans vs. 39 percent of Democrats). This gap on whether it is hard to tell what constitutes sexual harassment has widened by sixteen percentage points since 2017."[28]

The bottom line is that #MeToo has devolved from a movement that was meant to address a real social ill into something that can affect women in the workplace, lacks focus, and has become the subject of partisan division.

THE #METOO MOVEMENT CAN DO MORE TO ERADICATE THE CULTURE THAT ENABLES SEXUAL HARASSMENT

Many women believe that #MeToo has not gone far enough to change the culture that enables sexual harassment. They view efforts to push back against #MeToo as dishonest, and as an attempt to limit, attack, and undermine the women who seek change.

"The attacks come in all shapes and forms—targeting an individual's personal account of harm, a workplace's initiative, a researcher's methodology, or a government policy," write Diane White and Paula McDonald in *The*

> ***"We must have zero tolerance for sexual harassment, even if the perpetrator is somebody we like and admire."[29]***
>
> ***—Ana Navarro, political commentator***

In 1998, President Bill Clinton was impeached in part due to his consensual sexual affair with a twenty-two-year-old White House intern, Monica Lewinsky. At the time, approximately two-thirds of all Americans supported the president remaining in office. Today, Clinton would probably not have same level of support, thanks to cultural changes brought about by the #MeToo Movement.

Guardian. "These attacks are often insidious, with the fear of losing power dressed up as a legitimate concern about 'reverse discrimination' or 'an attack on fair process.' The loud voices of those who hold the power invariably come forward under the guise of hailing a return to sensible, rational discussion; returning balance to a debate that has tipped 'too far' in the favour of the 'feminist agenda.'"[30]

White and McDonald, like other supporters, contend that as the #MeToo Movement is necessary as long as women are afraid that if they report sexual harassment, they will suffer retribution in the workplace, and as long as powerful men are allowed to get away with their behavior. The #MeToo Movement is necessary to teach girls and young women that they do not need to submit to such treatment by men.

David Roberts, writing in *Vox*, suggests that sexual harassment and discrimination is not just a problem but a crisis—the severity of which most people, especially men,

Young girls participate in a Woman's March in Asbury Park, New Jersey. It is essential to create a society in which girls and young women are empowered and free from harassment.

do not understand. "Sexual discrimination, harassment, and abuse are everywhere," Roberts writes. "They are not isolated cases, not rare, and not confined to the powerful or famous. They constitute an ongoing, systemic crisis. #MeToo is meant to draw attention to that crisis. Talking about the perpetrators 'moving on with their lives' at all, much less with sympathy and solicitude, is a clear signal that the moral weight and severity of the crisis has not sunk in. We're still not taking this ... seriously."[31]

When a person believes that they have been sexually harassed, the first step would be to let the other person know that their behavior is offensive. Experts say that in many sexual harassment cases, the people responsible may not realize they are creating a hostile work environment. Raising concerns about their conduct may be enough to resolve the problem. If the problem continues after putting a harasser on notice, then the next step involves following the company's or institution's procedures for reporting sexual harassment. If that does not resolve the matter, the next step would be to file a report with the Equal Employment Opportunity Commission, or an equivalent state government agency. The last resort, but a powerful one nevertheless, is to file a lawsuit.

The way to end sexual harassment, and change the culture that permits it, is for victims to take action at once. #MeToo is performing a vital and necessary function, because suffering in silence only perpetuates the problem.

TEXT-DEPENDENT QUESTIONS

1. Who was Carmita Wood and what did she do?
2. What did the court case *Meritor Savings Bank v. Vinson* decide?
3. How did the #MeToo movement start?

RESEARCH PROJECTS

Investigate what the procedures are to file a complaint of sexual harassment, either at the Equal Employment Opportunity Commission (EEOC) or at a comparable agency in your state.

WORDS TO UNDERSTAND

abortion—the termination of a pregnancy with the death of the embryo or fetus.

embryo—the developing human individual from the time of implantation to the end of the eighth week after conception.

fetus—a developing human from usually eight weeks after conception to birth.

CHAPTER 4

SHOULD ABORTION BE MADE ILLEGAL?

No issue in recent American history has been so contentious as that of **abortion**. Since the landmark Supreme Court case *Roe v. Wade* made abortion a legal procedure in all fifty states, the two sides of the issue have been locked in a long struggle: the pro-choice side to keep abortion legal and the pro-life side to outlaw it.

According to the National Abortion Federation, a pro-choice group, in the decades before *Roe v. Wade*, the estimates of illegal abortions ranged as high as 1.2 million per year. "Many women died or suffered serious medical problems after attempting to self-induce their abortions or going to untrained practitioners who performed abortions with primitive methods or in unsanitary conditions," the organization notes. "During this time, hospital emergency room staff treated thousands of women who either died or were suffering terrible effects of abortions provided without adequate skill and care."[32] Wealthier women were able to obtain abortions from private doctors, although this was still illegal.

As the women's rights movement developed In the late 1960s and early 1970s, one-third of the states liberalized or repealed laws that prohibited abortion. In other states, women filed lawsuits challenging the restrictive laws.

In 1972, two young attorneys, Sarah Weddington and Linda Coffee, challenged the abortion law governing the state of Texas. They based their case on the Fourteenth Amendment, arguing that it guaranteed a woman's right to privacy. They maintained that whether a woman carried a pregnancy through to delivery or terminated the pregnancy was her own, private decision. The case, known as *Roe v. Wade*, eventually reached the U.S. Supreme Court.

On January 22, 1973, the Supreme Court, by a vote of seven to two, issued its ruling in *Roe v. Wade*, finding that all state laws barring or restricting abortions during the first three months of pregnancy violated a woman's fundamental right to privacy. Writing for the majority,

Scan here to learn about Alabama's controversial 2019 abortion law.

Justice Harry Blackmun said the right to privacy—which had been established in a previous case, *Griswold v. Connecticut* (1965)—"is broad enough to encompass a woman's decision whether or not to terminate her pregnancy."[33]

According to the Alan Guttmacher Institute, a New York–based foundation that studies reproductive health issues and advocates for abortion rights, in 1973, after the *Roe v. Wade* decision, there were some 744,000 abortions performed in the United States. By 1975 the number of

WHO WERE ROE AND WADE?

The plaintiff in the *Roe v. Wade* case was Norma McCorvey, a twenty-one-year-old waitress who had become pregnant. Due to the publicity surrounding the case, her name was changed in court documents to "Jane Roe," in order to protect her privacy. Henry Wade was the Texas attorney general, who defended the state law that made abortions illegal.

Ironically, later in her life Norma McCorvey came to regret her involvement in the case. She became a fervent pro-life activist in the mid-1990s, and remained active in the pro-life movement until her death in 2017.

abortions performed in the United States exceeded 1 million.

Americans remain deeply divided by the issue of abortion. Vocal (some would say extremist) minorities have staked out uncompromising positions as "pro-choice" (supporting unfettered abortion rights for women) or "pro-life" (opposed to abortion under any circumstance). These groups maintain a steady stream of shrill rhetoric while frequently demonizing those who support the other side. Meanwhile, opinion polls conducted since the 1970s show that most Americans continue to fall somewhere in the middle on the abortion issue, accepting a women's right to have an abortion, but also recognizing certain limitations on that right.

One reason the controversy has persisted is that abortion was made legal by a Supreme Court decision and not a federal statute. The procedure cannot become illegal unless a constitutional amendment is passed declaring a baby a human being from conception—an unlikely process—or if the Supreme Court reverses itself. The latter fact has made almost every Supreme Court confirmation a horrendous, bare-knuckle fight. A conservative court might just tilt toward reversing *Roe v. Wade* and allowing the states to outlaw abortion again.

A peaceful "March for Life" takes place in Washington every year on the anniversary of the Roe v. Wade decision.

HUMAN LIFE BEGINS AT CONCEPTION, SO ABORTION SHOULD BE OUTLAWED EXCEPT IN EXTREME CASES

One of the main arguments against legal abortion stems from a belief that a child is a human being from the moment of conception. It therefore follows that terminating a pregnancy results in killing that human being—in other words, murder.

"The first argument against abortion takes as its starting point a profoundly humanistic premise: Every single human life has an inherent 'dignity' or excellence," notes a statement by the Roman Catholic Church. "This dignity is not based upon performance; one does not have to qualify for this excellence. Nor is this dignity the reward of others, be it the state or one's parents. Rather, this dignity stems from one's very nature as a rational being made in the image of God. All possessors of human nature are valuable—no exceptions. How valuable? Irreplaceably valuable, since each human is unique.

"If one accepts this premise, then the logic of the argument is inescapable. The unborn child is without doubt human. She possesses her own unique DNA, and she develops her own skeletal system, organs and appendages. While reliant upon her mother for nutrition, she is in no way a mere 'part' of her mother's body. To intentionally kill such a human being in the womb, as occurs in abortion, is a horrific offense against human dignity, a failure to respect a being of inestimable value."[35]

The Catholic Church makes another argument,

stemming from the loss of human potential that abortion causes. "The already-existing child in the womb has the potential to develop in various ways and to accomplish certain things, and abortion absolutely nullifies these

The Roman Catholic Church has taken a leading role in the pro-life movement. Other Christian denominations, as well as religions like Judaism and Hinduism also tend to oppose abortion unless carrying the baby would put the mother's life at risk.

potentialities. As the Radiance Foundation succinctly made this point, 'She can do super things if she is born.'"

"Life is the good that is at the foundation of other goods. In destroying the life of a child, we also destroy the additional good things in the future that would flow from her life."[38]

FATHERS' RIGHTS AND ABORTION

Fathers essentially have no rights where it comes to the question of whether or not their partners can have an abortion. The father's consent is not legally required, and a woman can choose to terminate a pregnancy whether or not the father agrees.

"The Supreme Court has found laws requiring a spouse's consent for an abortion to be unconstitutional," notes FindLaw.com. "In *Planned Parenthood v. Danforth*, the Court reasoned that a husband's refusal to consent would in effect veto a woman's choice to terminate a pregnancy. While both prospective fathers and pregnant women have an interest in the decision, when the two disagree, only one partner's position can prevail. According to the Court, since the woman actually carries the pregnancy, 'the balance weighs in her favor,' preventing the husband from vetoing her choice."[36]

Some pro-life activists cite scientific arguments against abortion. Advances in neo-natal medicine since *Roe v. Wade* was decided in the 1970s are used to support the view that a **fetus** is a human being at the moment of conception. They argue that the earliest developmental stages of the human **embryo** are all made up of human DNA and human cells, so it is undeniably human.

The National Center for Biotechnology Information suggests that an abortion can have lasting mental and

Some states have tried to pass laws that require married women to inform their husbands before having an abortion. However, the Supreme Court has struck down such laws, following the same reasoning about protecting the rights of women. "The Supreme Court addressed this question in *Planned Parenthood v. Casey* and found that such a law was unconstitutional," notes FindLaw.com. "While most women discuss an abortion with their partners, those who don't were much more likely to be in abusive relationships, according to the Court. The Supreme Court saw spousal notification requirements as placing an undue burden on women who may fear for their safety, or that of their children."[37]

> ***"The greatest destroyer of peace is abortion because if a mother can kill her own child, what is left for me to kill you and you to kill me? There is nothing between."[34]***
>
> ***—Mother Teresa, humanitarian***

physical health effects on women who undergo them.

"There have been a number of studies that have tried to prove that abortion is not harmful to a woman's state of mind. However, the flaws of these studies include: the lack of controlled studies where abortions are randomized as a treatment for pregnancy; not taking into account the woman's state of mind before the pregnancy; use of questionnaires to gain information on well-suppressed feelings; and few studies with comparison groups. It has also been discovered that women who had elective abortions suffered higher psychological trauma than women who gave birth to stillborn children. However, emotional distress was found to be higher among women that had repeat abortions. In other studies, it was found that women who had previous abortions and were looking forward to being pregnant were more anxious about the pregnancy than women who had never had abortions. Recent studies on women that have had abortions show that they run a greater risk of complications such as: eclampsia, bleeding, miscarriage, maternal mortality and post-partum complications. Past abortions may also have an effect on the relationship which exists between the mother and surviving children."[39]

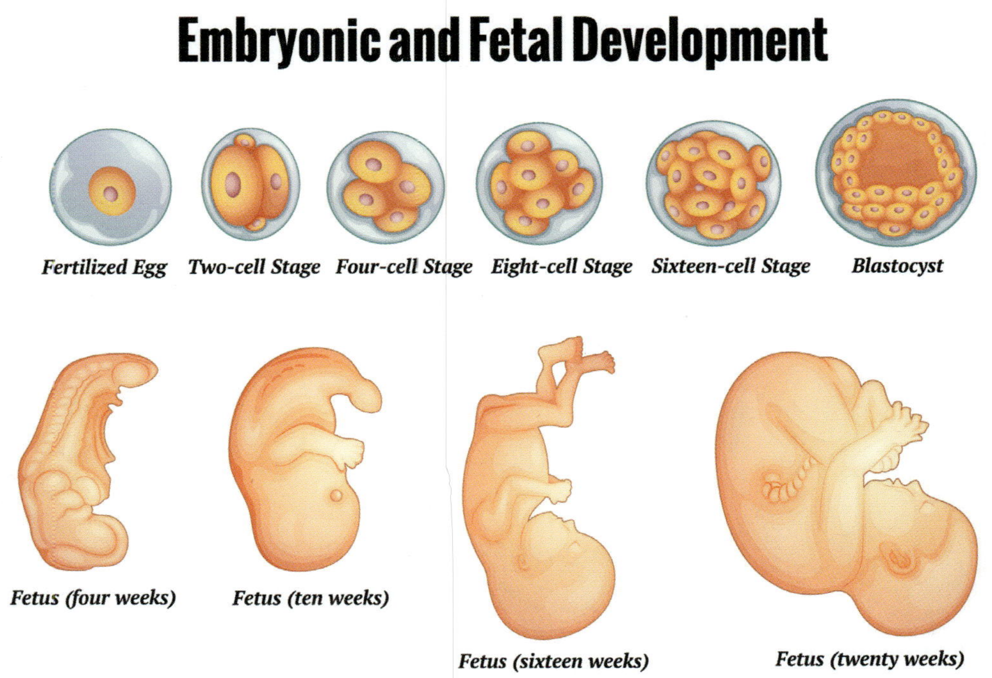

ABORTION SHOULD REMAIN LEGAL, TO PRESERVE WOMEN'S AUTONOMY OVER THEIR OWN BODIES

The right to an abortion should be recognized as a fundamental right, because of the great impact childbearing has on a woman's life. Unwanted pregnancies disrupt the mother's life, imposing a financial burden and forcing women to go through the physical experience of

A teenager who becomes pregnant accidentally may seek an abortion, believing that having a baby will have a major impact on her life.

pregnancy and childbirth. In many cases, there is also the psychological and social stigma of being an unwed mother.

Laws that restrict womens' access to abortion infringe on Americans' right to privacy, enshrined in the Constitution. Government interest in protecting the mother's health does not justify a total ban on abortions, only regulation to increase the safety of such a procedure. In addition, "persons" elsewhere in the Constitution clearly refers to persons after birth, as in the enumeration (or census) clause—not to unborn fetuses.

"You cannot have maternal health without reproductive health. And reproductive health includes contraception and family planning and access to legal, safe abortion."[43]

—Hillary Clinton, American politician

The *UCLA Law Review* suggests that there is a gender equality argument for keeping abortion legal. "Equality arguments for abortion rights range widely but share certain core concerns," notes an article. "Sex equality arguments ask whether abortion restrictions are shaped solely by the state's interest in protecting potential life, or whether such laws might also reflect constitutionally suspect judgments about women. For example, does the state act consistently to protect potential life outside the abortion context, including by offering prenatal care and job protections to women who want to become mothers? Or is the state selective in protecting potential life? If so, might abortion restrictions reflect traditional sex-role stereotypes about sex, caregiving, or decision-making around motherhood?"[40] The article continues:

> Equality arguments are also concerned about the gendered impact of abortion restrictions. Sex equality arguments observe that abortion restrictions deprive women of control over the timing of motherhood and so predictably exacerbate the inequalities in educational, economic, and political life engendered by childbearing and childrearing. Sex equality arguments ask whether, in protecting unborn life, the state has taken steps to ameliorate the effects of compelled motherhood on women, or whether the state has proceeded with indifference to the impact of its actions on women. Liberty arguments focus less on these gendered biases and burdens on women.[41]

Men, after all, do not have to deal with the physical and psychological burdens of pregnancy. The burden is all on the woman.

In an opinion piece on CNN, Danielle Campoamor

In 2019, new state laws related to abortion in Alabama and New York inflamed activists on both sides of the issue.

suggests that overturning *Roe v. Wade* would force many women to seek abortions illegally, which would result in an increase in deaths. "It is inherently violent to call for the demolition of *Roe v. Wade* and wish to return to a time when abortion was listed as the official cause of death for almost 2,700 women in the United States.... It's violent to continue to introduce anti-abortion restrictions when a 2017 study conducted by Ibis Reproductive Health and the Center for Reproductive Rights found that states with the highest abortion restrictions also have the highest maternal mortality and infant mortality rates. According to UN experts, repealing anti-abortion laws would save the lives of nearly 50,000 women a year."[42]

TEXT-DEPENDENT QUESTIONS

1. What did *Roe v. Wade* decide?
2. What is the DNA argument that a fetus is a human being from the moment of conception?
3. What is the gender equality argument for keeping abortion legal?

RESEARCH PROJECTS

Research the organizations and resources available in your community that can assist a woman who has an unplanned pregnancy. They can be abortion providers as well as organizations that will help with neo-natal care and, if chosen, the subsequent

WORDS TO UNDERSTAND

implicit bias—unconsciously held assumptions or associations about members of a particular ethnic or social group.

pervasive—something that is widespread.

trajectory—the curved path that a flying body, such as a planet or a rocket, follows in space.

CHAPTER 5

DOES DISCRIMINATION PREVENT WOMEN FROM GOING INTO STEM FIELDS?

The history of American women in fields of science, technology, engineering, and mathematics (STEM), contains many inspiring stories. Some notable Americans include Grace Hopper, who helped to develop the first commercial computer UNIVAC; Rachel Carson, a marine biologist whose book *Silent Spring* helped to launch the environmental movement; Edith Clarke, a pioneering electrical engineer and inventor; Katherine Johnson, an African-American mathematician whose helped calculate the **trajectories** for NASA's manned space missions from the 1960s until the 1980s; and Margaret Hamilton, a computer scientist who was one of the first software engineers. But these women were the exception rather than the rule.

The shortage of girls and women in STEM fields, at least earlier in American history, can be ascribed to attitudes about gender roles. Until the twentieth century, most women were expected to stay at home, raise the children, and do the cleaning and cooking. However, during World

War II, the need for scientists and engineers collided with a shortage of men due to military service, and so programs were started to train women in science and engineering.

After the war, it became harder for women to get science or engineering jobs. Returning soldiers went to school on the GI Bill, and were soon getting the higher-paying scientific jobs over the women who had been trained to work in the scientific fields during the war.

During the Cold War—and particularly after the Soviet Union launched its Sputnik satellites in the fall of 1957—the US government pushed for the American educational system to produce more graduates in the STEM fields. Unfortunately, the need for STEM education conflicted with the gender norms and discrimination against working women that was common in the 1960s. But some female

To learn about some women who changed science forever, scan here.

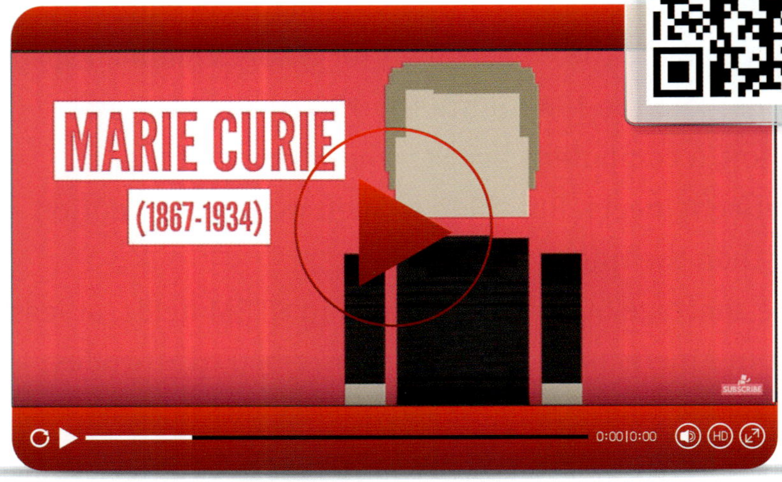

scientists, engineers, and educators were able to help women succeed in STEM fields even before the Women's Rights Movement made issues of employment equity and gender stereotyping part of the national conversation.

Today, decades after the height of the Cold War, women in the workplace is an accepted fact. However, the gender

In 1958, Mary Jackson became NASA's first black female engineer. She had graduated with the highest honors from high school, then earned degrees in mathematics and physical science from Hampton Institute. She worked for NASA as an aeronautical engineer for thirty-four years.

Grace Hopper was a pioneer of computer programming. After earning a Ph.D. in mathematics at Yale University, she was a teacher until World War II, when she joined the US Navy Reserve. She helped to develop UNIVAC I, the first computer sold for commercial use, as well as the COBOL programming language, which is still in use today.

gap in STEM persists. "Women remain underrepresented in the science and engineering workforce, although to a lesser degree than in the past, with the greatest disparities occurring in engineering, computer science, and the physical sciences," notes a 2016 report by the National Girls Collaborative Project. "Women make up half of the total U.S. college-educated workforce, but only 29 percent of the science and engineering workforce. Female scientists and engineers are concentrated in different occupations than are men, with relatively high shares of women in the social sciences (62 percent) and biological, agricultural, and environmental life sciences (48 percent) and relatively low shares in engineering (15 percent) and computer and mathematical sciences (25 percent)."[44]

The reason for this continuing gap is hotly debated. Some people believe a culture of discrimination, perhaps unconscious, still exists in the STEM fields. Others argue that sociological and even psychological factors have something to do with it. The essays that follow will examine both sides of this matter.

DISCRIMINATION MUST BE ADDRESSED TO CLOSE THE STEM GAP

While overt discrimination seems to be a thing of the past in the STEM fields, certain stereotypes remain that can subtly effect female performance. For example, there is a **pervasive** myth that "women are not good at math." Many people say that they don't believe this stereotype. However, even confident women can still hold that belief at an unconscious level. "These unconscious beliefs, or **implicit biases**, may be more powerful than explicitly

> ***"Certain people—men, of course—discouraged me, saying [science] was not a good career for women. That pushed me even more to persevere."[45]***
>
> ***—Francoise Barre, virologist and winner of the 2008 Nobel Prize in Physiology and Medicine***

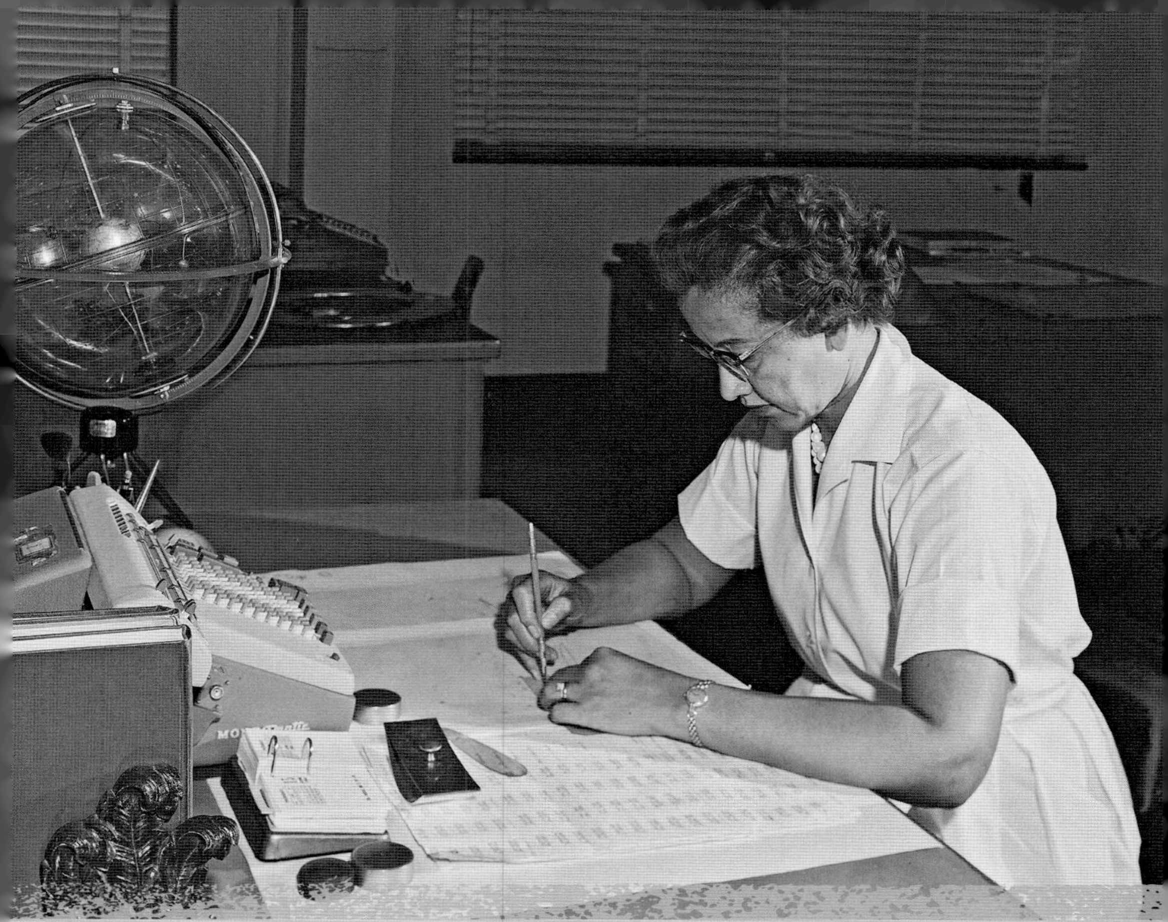

Mathematician Katherine G. Johnson was a "human computer" who helped to plot trajectories for America's first manned space missions, made calculations that enabled the Project Apollo moon landings, and worked on the space shuttle in the 1970s and 1980s. She wrote or co-wrote twenty-six major research reports during her more than thirty years working for NASA.

held beliefs and values simply because we are not aware of them," notes the American Association of University Women (AAUW). "Even if overt gender bias is waning, as some argue, research shows that unconscious beliefs underlying negative stereotypes continue to influence assumptions about people and behavior."[46]

Although women earn more bachelor's degrees than men each year, they are underrepresented in specific STEM fields, including computer science, engineering, and mathematics.

The American Association of University Women has developed some suggestions on how to counteract these biases and get more girls and women interested in science and engineering. One of their suggestions is to educate people about women's achievements in math and science, to help eliminate unfair stereotypes. Another is to teach all students about the danger of believing stereotypes. Elementary and high school curricula should teach girls that intellectual skills are acquired, and encourage all children to develop their spatial skills. Talented and gifted programs should send the message that they value growth and learning, and girls in high school should be encouraged to take calculus, physics, chemistry, computer science, and engineering classes when available.

At the college level, the AAUW recommends that schools should actively recruit women into STEM majors, and emphasize real-life applications in early STEM courses. Colleges and universities should take proactive steps to support women STEM majors.

For example, sponsor social events to help integrate women into the department, provide a student lounge open to all students to encourage interaction outside of class, or sponsor a women's associations for each STEM major, such as "Women in Biology" or "Women in Computer Science." Title IX requires schools that receive federal funding to provide programs in which women have the same opportunities as men in science, technology, engineering, and math. Professors at institutes of higher education can also be trained to be aware of the danger of stereotypes.

For STEM graduates who are entering academic fields, there are other things that can be done. Department chairs should conduct period reviews, to assess the climate for female faculty. New faculty members should have mentors to work with, and schools or institutions should support faculty work-life balance with stop-tenure-clock policies and on-site child care.

The National Association for the Gifted and Talented suggests that one part of the problem is a lack of confidence in young women in their abilities, plus a gender-related preference in preferred fields of study. "While women make up over 57 percent of college graduates, only 14.8 percent of engineers in the workforce are women," notes an NAGT study. "Many women will change out of engineering majors during college as they find the fields uninviting or unappealing during their college years. And, while female engineering majors perform academically just as well as men, they have a tendency to underrate their technical abilities." The study continues:

> Women seem to be more attracted to sciences that are behavioral and biological, while computer science, physics, and engineering are overwhelmingly male. Only 7 percent of mechanical engineers, 12 percent of civil engineers, 15 percent of chemical engineers, and 13 percent of aerospace engineers are women."[47]

The NAGT suggests that positive feedback and encouragement are needed to get women and girls more interested in STEM fields.

In *Forbes*, Amy Blankson, a Harvard and Yale School of Management graduate, suggests that lack of mentoring by male supervisors and professors may play a part in the STEM gender gap.

"Those working diligently in this field realize that recruiting the next generation of girls into STEM careers has to go beyond pure inspiration and delve into systemic barriers as well," writes Blankson. "For instance, [Emily] Calandrelli admits that her STEM classes often felt like an 'all-boys club.' She was often one of two or three females in a class of fifty students, which left her feeling less supported than her peers. She explains, 'Because most of my professors and bosses were male, it was difficult to receive the same valuable one-on-one mentorship time due to stigmas associated with older men hanging out with younger women. Some male mentors were afraid of what people would think by spending time with a young female student but didn't think twice spending that same time with a male student.'"[48]

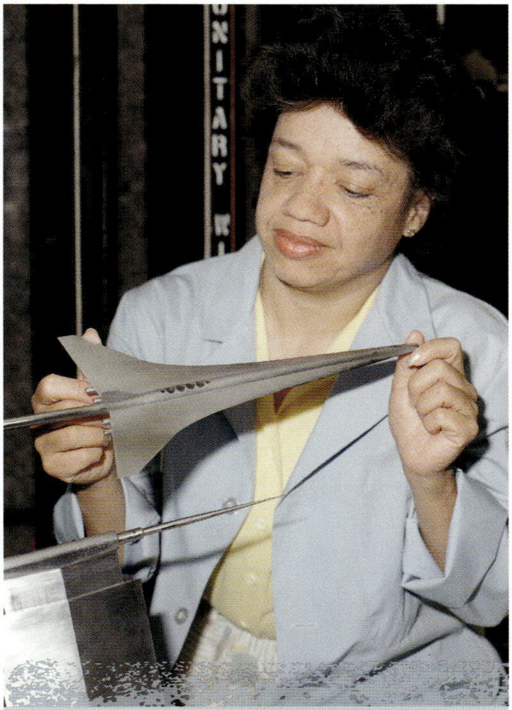

American mathematician and data analyst Dr. Christine Darden became one of the world's foremost experts on supersonic flight.

Closing the STEM gender gap will take a systematic change in attitudes of both men and women. Men must become more accepting of female scientists and engineers. Women need to develop more self-confidence in their abilities in science and math.

DISCRIMINATION DOES NOT CAUSE THE STEM GENDER GAP

The STEM gender gap has less to do with discrimination against women than it does with women's choices. A recent study in *Psychological Science* indicates that in the countries that offer the least freedom to women, such as Arab states like Jordan, Qatar, and the United Arab Emirates, women are more likely to choose STEM fields in college than are women in western liberal democracies, where they have greater freedom and equality to men.

> ***"What everyone in the astronaut corps shares in common is not gender or ethnic background, but motivation, perseverance, and desire—the desire to participate in a voyage of discovery."[49]***
>
> ***—Dr. Ellen Ochoa, engineer and NASA astronaut***

Unlike in countries that restrict women's rights, women in the United States are free to choose a career field that they find to be the most fulfilling or personally satisfying.

The study authors Gijsbert Stoet and David Geary concluded that this occurs because women in countries with higher gender inequality are seeking the clearest possible path to financial freedom. Often, that path leads through STEM professions.

"The countries that minted the most female college graduates in fields like science, engineering, or math were also some of the least gender-equal countries. They posit that this is because the countries that empower women

In September 1992, Dr. Mae C. Jemison became the first African-American woman in space. A medical doctor who once served with the Peace Corps in Sierra Leone, Africa, Jemison spent more than 190 hours in space.

also empower them, indirectly, to pick whatever career they'd enjoy most and be best at," notes an article about the study. "Countries with the highest gender equality tend to be welfare states with a high level of social security."[50]

Meanwhile, less gender-equal countries tend to also have less social support for people who find themselves out of work. Stoet and Geary suggest that young women in those countries are more likely to enter STEM professions because they offer a more certain financial future than careers in other subjects. Women in western countries like the United States choose not go into STEM fields because they find more satisfaction in other careers such as business, law, writing, or the arts. In places where women don't have such options, STEM may be their best choice.

Other recent studies have indicated that there truly is no gender gap in STEM education in the United States. "According to several measures, women are actually slightly over-represented in STEM graduate programs and earn a majority of STEM college degrees," notes a recent paper by the American Enterprise Institute. "A lot depends on how we define 'Science, Technology, Engineering and Math (STEM)' and that definition is fairly fluid and subject to various interpretations. According to the Bureau of Labor Statistics 'The definition of STEM can vary, depending on the group using it.'"[51]

As it turns out, when one measures graduate school enrollment number, more women (50,965) than men (42,477) studied biological and agricultural sciences in

2017, the most recent year for which complete data is available. The numbers are even starker in health and medical science, where 186,869 women were enrolled in graduate programs, compared to 53,147 men. However, men still outnumber women in engineering, math and computer science, and earth and physical science.

If society believes that there would be a benefit to having more women involved in STEM fields outside of medicine, then achieving that goal is more complicated than "consciousness raising" to remove a bias that doesn't exist. Some other way must be found to persuade more young women that STEM fields can be just as fulfilling, if not more so, than other courses of study.

One idea is to encourage girls' interest in math, science and computers at an early age, and built their confidence and enjoyment of science and math. But even this approach might not help to change girls' interests. "The fact is that men and women say they want to do different types of jobs," write Stoet and Geary. ""If you're interested in increasing the happiness of a society, you have to accept that men and women do different things."[52]

TEXT-DEPENDENT QUESTIONS

1. Why did World War II see an upsurge in the number of women in STEM fields?
2. What are the two main reasons for increasing the number of women in STEM careers?
3. Name two STEM areas where more women than men are working?

RESEARCH PROJECTS

Select a famous women scientist and engineer. Write a brief essay about what she accomplished, mentioning what if any institutional or cultural bias she had to overcome.

SERIES GLOSSARY OF KEY TERMS

affidavit—a sworn statement, in writing, that sets out a person's testimony.

affirmative action programs—programs that are intended to improve the educational or employment opportunities of members of minority groups and women.

BCE and CE—alternatives to the traditional Western designation of calendar eras, which used the birth of Jesus as a dividing line. BCE stands for "Before the Common Era," and is equivalent to BC ("Before Christ"). Dates labeled CE, or "Common Era," are equivalent to Anno Domini (AD, or "the Year of Our Lord").

colony—a country or region ruled by another country.

democracy—a country in which the people can vote to choose those who govern them.

discrimination—prejudiced outlook, action, or treatment, often in a negative way.

detention center—a place where people claiming asylum and refugee status are held while their case is investigated.

ethnic cleansing—an attempt to rid a country or region of a particular ethnic group. The term was first used to describe the attempt by Serb nationalists to rid Bosnia of Muslims.

felony—a serious crime; in the United States, a felony is any crime for which the punishment is more than one year in prison or the death penalty.

fundamentalist—beliefs based on a strict biblical or scriptural interpretation of religious law.

median—In statistics, the number that falls in the center of a group, meaning half the numbers are higher than the number and half are lower.

minority—a part of a population different from the majority in some characteristics and often subjected to differential treatment.

paranoia—a mental disorder characterized by the strong belief that the person is being unfairly persecuted.

parole—releasing someone sentenced to prison before the full sentence is served, granted for good behavior.

plaintiff—a person making a complaint in a legal case in civil court.

pro bono—a Latin phrase meaning "for the public good," referring to legal work undertaken without payment or at a reduced fee as a public service.

racial profiling—projecting the characteristics of a few people onto the entire population of a group; for example, when police officers stop people on suspicion of criminal activity solely because of their race.

racism—discrimination against a particular group of people based solely on their racial background.

segregation—the separation or isolation of a race, class, or group from others in society. This can include restricting areas in which members of the race, class, or group can live; placing barriers to social interaction; separate educational facilities; or other discriminatory means.

ORGANIZATIONS TO CONTACT

American Association
of University Women
1310 L Street NW, Suite 1000
Washington, DC 20005
Phone: (800) 326-2289
Website: www.aauw.org

Center for Reproductive Rights
199 Water Street
New York, NY 10038
Phone: (917) 637-3600
Fax: (917) 637-3666
Website: www.reproductiverights.org

Emily's List
1800 M Street NW, Suite 375N
Washington, DC 20036
Phone: (800) 68-EMILY
Website: www.emilyslist.org

Equality Now
125 Maiden Lane, 9th Floor, Suite B
New York NY 10038
Phone: (212) 586-0906
Fax: (212) 586-1611
Website: www.equalitynow.org

Girls on the Run International
801 East Morehead Street, Suite 201
Charlotte, NC 28202
Phone: (800) 901-9965
Website: www.girlsontherun.org

League of Women Voters
1730 M Street NW, Suite 1000,
Washington, DC 20036
Phone: (202) 429-1965
Website: www.lwv.org

National Organization for Women
1100 H Street NW, Suite 300
Washington, DC 20005
Phone (202) 628-8669
Website: https://now.org

Susan B. Anthony List
2800 Shirlington Road, Suite 1200
Arlington, VA 22206
Phone: (202) 223-8073
Email: information@sbalist.org
Website: www.sba-list.org

US Women's Chamber of Commerce
700 12th Street NW, Suite 700
Washington, DC 20005
Phone: (202) 607-2488
Website: www.uswcc.org

FURTHER READING

Collins, Gail. *When Everything Changed: The Amazing Journey of American Women from 1960 to Present*. New York: Little, Brown, and Co., 2009.

Dolan, Catherine. *The Not So Sexy Truth: Women, Men, and Sexual Harassment in the Workplace*. New York: Motivational Press, 2018.

Friedan, Betty. *Life So Far: A Memoir*. New York: Simon & Schuster, 2000.

Gilligan, Carol. *In a Different Voice: Psychological Theory and Women's Development*. Boston: Harvard University Press, 2016.

Humphrey, Elizabeth King. *The Feminist Movement Today*. Philadelphia: Mason Crest, 2013.

McMillen, Sally G. *Seneca Falls and the Origins of the Women's Rights Movement*. New York: Oxford University Press, 2008.

Norton, Mary Beth, and Ruth M. Alexander, eds. *Major Problems in American Women's History*, 4th ed. Boston: Houghton Mifflin, 2007.

Sanger, Carol. *About Abortion: Terminating Pregnancy in Twenty-First-Century America*. New York: Belnap Press, 2017.

Shetterly, Margot Lee. *Hidden Figures: The American Dream and the Untold Story of the Black Women Mathematicians Who Helped Win the Space Race*. New York: William Morrow, 2016.

Swaby, Rachal. *Headstrong: 52 Women Who Changed Science-and the World*. New York: Broadway Books, 2015.

INTERNET RESOURCES

https://iwpr.org
The Institute for Women's Policy Research studies and disseminates information on policy issues concerning women.

https://nwlc.org/issues/
The National Women's Law Center advances women's rights through litigation and public policy proposals.

www.cfa.harvard.edu/~srugheimer/Women_in_STEM_Resources.html
This page is a compendium of resources for women to enter STEM fields, provided by Harvard University

http://womenincongress.house.gov
This site provides information about female members of Congress, past and present.

http://www.womensmemorial.org/Education/timeline.html
A timeline of American women in military service, from the Revolutionary War to the present.

http://www.now.org
The home page of the National Organization for Women (NOW).

https://www.heritage.org/life
The Heritage Foundation is a conservative-oriented think tank that tends to take a free market view on economic issues.

http://www.aei.org/tag/womens-rights
The American Enterprise Institute is a conservative think tank that studies issues of public policy, including women's rights and the wage gap.

CHAPTER NOTES

[1] National Women's History Alliance, "Timeline of Legal History of Women in the United States," (accessed April 2019). http://www.nwhp.org/resources/womens-rights-movement/detailed-timeline/

[2] Letter from Abigail Adams to John Adams, 31 March–5 April 1776, Massachusetts Historical Society (accessed April 2019). https://www.masshist.org/digitaladams/archive/doc?id=L17760331aa

[3] Dr. Graham Warder, "Women In Nineteenth-Century America," Keene State College (accessed April 2019). https:// socialwelfare.library.vcu.edu/woman-suffrage/women-in-nineteenth-century-america-2/

[4] Dr. Graham Warder, "Women In Nineteenth-Century America."

[5] Dr. Graham Warder, "Women In Nineteenth-Century America."

[6] Biography.com, "Margaret Sanger," (accessed April 2019). https://www.biography.com/people/margaret-sanger-9471186

[7] Gloria Steinem, quoted in Claire Warner, "17 Inspiring Quotes About Women's Equality For Women's Equality Day, Because We've Made A Lot Of Progress, Even If We Aren't There Yet," Bustle (August 26, 2015). https://www.bustle.com/articles/106640-17-inspiring-quotes-about-womens-equality-for-womens- equality-day-because-weve-made-a-lot-of

[8] Sandra Day O'Connor, "Remarks at Senior Roundtable for Women's Justice," U.S. State Department archive (March 12, 2008). https://2001-2009.state.gov/secretary/rm/ 2008/03/102147.htm

[9] The History Channel, "Women's Suffrage," (accessed April 2019). https://www.history.com/topics/womens-history/the- fight-for-womens-suffrage

[10] Encyclopedia Britannica, "Women's Rights Movement," (accessed April 2019). https://www.britannica.com/topic/ womens-movement

[11] Susan B. Anthony, quoted in *Votes for Women: Complete History of the Women's Suffrage Movement* (New York: Madison and Adams Press, 2018).

[12] Christina Hoff Sommers, "The War Against Boys," *The Atlantic* (May 2000). https:// www.theatlantic.com/magazine/archive/2000/05/the-war-against-boys/304659/

[13] Institute for Women's Policy Research, "Pay Equity and Discrimination," (accessed April 2019). https://iwpr.org/issue/ employment-education-economic-change/pay-equity-discrimination/

[14] S 2199: Paycheck Fairness Act, Congress.gov. https://www.congress.gov/bill/113th-congress/ senate-bill/2199

[15] American Bar Association, "The Paycheck Fairness Act," (accessed April 2019). https://www.americanbar.org/ advocacy/governmental_legislative_

work/priorities_policy/discrimination/the-paycheck- fairness-act/

[16] Megyn Kelly, quoted in Evgenia Peretz, "Blowhards, Beware: Megyn Kelly Will Slay You Now," *Vanity Fair* (February 2016). https://www.vanityfair.com/news/2015/12/z-kelly-fox-news- cover-story

[17] Christina Hoff Sommers, "Fair Pay Isn't Always Equal Pay," *New York Times* (September 21, 2010). https://www.nytimes.com/2010/09/22/opinion/22Sommers.html

[18] CONSAD Research Corp, "An Analysis of Reasons for the Disparity in Wages Between Men and Women," (accessed April 2019). https://www.shrm.org/hr-today/public-policy/hr-public-policy-issues/Documents/ Gender%20Wage%20Gap%20Final%20Report.pdf

[19] National Organization for Women, "The Paycheck Fairness Act Would Finally Assure Equal Pay for Equal Work," (accessed April 2019). https://now.org/media-center/press-release/the-paycheck-fairness-act-would-finally-assure-equal-pay-for-equal-work/

[20] Sascha Cohen, "A Brief History of Sexual Harassment in America Before Anita Hill," *Time* (April 11, 2016). http://time.com/4286575/sexual-harassment-before-anita-hill/

[21] Cohen, "A Brief History of Sexual Harassment in America Before Anita Hill."

[22] Cohen, "A Brief History of Sexual Harassment in America Before Anita Hill."

[23] Romeo Vitelli, Ph.D., "When Men Face Sexual Harassment," *Psychology Today* (May 11, 2015). https://www.psychologytoday.com/us/blog/media-spotlight/201505/when-men-face-sexual-harassment

[24] Vitelli, "When Men Face Sexual Harassment."

[25] Prudy Gourguechon, "Why In The World Would Men Stop Mentoring Women Post #MeToo?" *Forbes* (August 6, 2018). https://www.forbes.com/sites/prudygourguechon/2018/08/06/why-in-the-world-would-men-stop-mentoring-women-post-metoo/#631f83d179a5

[26] Cheryl Yeoh, quoted in Alanna Vagianos, "This CEO Hopes Her Story Can Change Silicon Valley's Culture Of Sexual Harassment," *Huffington Post* (July 7, 2017). https://www.huffingtonpost.com/entry/this-ceo-is- using-her-story-to-change-silicon-valleys-culture-of-sexual- harassment_us_595eb2bbe4b0d5b458e95adc? utm_campaign=hp_fb_pages&utm_source=women_fb&utm_medium=facebook&ncid=fcbklnku

[27] Megan Garber, "Is #MeToo Too Big?" *The Atlantic* (July 4, 2018). https://www.theatlantic.com/entertainment/archive/2018/07/is-metoo-too-big/564275/

CHAPTER NOTES

[28] Ipsos/NPR Examine Views on Sexual Harassment and Assault, Ipsos, October 31, 2018, https://www.ipsos.com/en-us/news-polls/NPR-Sexual-Harassment-and-Assault

[29] Ava Navarro, "Gables Police Chief Hudak Went to a Pool Party of Bikini-Clad Officers—and Did Nothing Wrong," *Miami Herald* (April 23, 2018). https://www.miamiherald.com/latest-news/article209640044.html

[30] Diane White and Paula McDonald, "As the Kavanaugh Backlash Shows, #MeToo Hasn't Gone Far Enough," *The Guardian* (October 4, 2018). https://www.theguardian.com/commentisfree/2018/oct/ 05/people-worry-metoo-has-gone-too-far-it-has-not-gone-far-enough

[31] David Roberts, "What So Many Men Are Missing About #MeToo," *Vox* (September 12, 2018). https:// www.vox.com/2018/9/10/17826168/me-too-louis-ck-men-comeback

[32] National Abortion Federation, "History of Abortion," (accessed June 2019). https://prochoice.org/education-and- advocacy/about-abortion/history-of-abortion/

[33] *Roe v. Wade* (U.S. Supreme Court 410 U.S. 113 (1973), majority opinion by Justice Harry Blackmun.

[34] Catholic News Agency, "Blessed Mother Theresa on Abortion," (February 5, 1994). https:// www.catholicnewsagency.com/resources/abortion/catholic-teaching/blessed-mother-teresa-on- abortion

[35] Alexander Schimpf, "Two Arguments Against Abortion," Roman Catholic Archdiocese of Oklahoma City (September 13, 2018). https:// archokc.org/news/two-arguments-against-abortion

[36] FindLaw, "Fathers' Rights and Abortion," (accessed June 2019). https://family.findlaw.com/paternity/fathers-rights-and-abortion.html

[37] FindLaw, "Father's Rights and Abortion."

[38] Schimpf, "Two Arguments Against Abortion."

[39] National Center for Biotechnology Information, "Mental Health and Abortion: Review and Analysis," (November 14, 1989). https://www.ncbi.nlm.nih.gov/pubmed/2682716

[40] Neil S. Siegel and Reva B. Siegel, "Equality Arguments for Abortion Rights," *UCLA Law Review* 160 (2013). https://www.uclalawreview.org/the-equality-argument-for-abortion-rights/

[41] Siegel and Siegel, "Equality Arguments for Abortion Rights."

[42] Danielle Campoamor, "Why Supporting Abortion Is a Pro-Life Position," CNN (May 5, 2018). https://www.cnn.com/2018/05/05/opinions/supporting-abortion-is-pro-life-opinion-campoamor/ index.html

[43] Hillary Clinton, "Transcript of Secretary Clinton's Statement to G8 Ministers," Center for Reproductive Rights (April 7, 2010). https://www.reproductiverights.org/feature/clinton-to-canada-abortion-access-must-be-included-in-g8-initiative#transcript

[44] National Girls Collaborative Project, "State of Girls and Women in STEM," (accessed June 2019). https:// ngcproject.org/statistics

[45] Francoise Barre, quoted in Lindsey H. Davis, "Forgotten Scientists," NIHR Imperial Patient Safety Translational Research Centre (February 11, 2017). https://wwwf.imperial.ac.uk/blog/pstrc/2017/02/11/forgotten- scientists/

[46] American Association of University Women, "Why So Few? Women in Science, Technology, Engineering, and Mathematics," (accessed June 2019). https://www.aauw.org/research/why-so-few/

[47] Barbara Swicord, "Five Ways to Close the Gender Gap in STEM Fields," National Society for the Gifted and Talented (March 7, 2017). https://www.nsgt.org/close-gender-gap-stem-fields/

[48] Amy Blankson, "Three Inspiring Role Models Embrace Modern Media To Close The STEM Gender Gap," Forbes (October 9, 2018). https://www.forbes.com/sites/amyblankson/2018/10/09/closing- the-stem-gap-with-modern-media-role-models/#185184bc5fd8

[49] Ellen Ochoa, quoted in Beth Brumbaugh, "Women's History Month Shout Out: Dr. Ellen Ochoa," Women@NASA blog (March 18, 2015). https://blogs.nasa.gov/womenatnasa/2015/03/18/womens-history-month-shout- out-dr-ellen-ochoa/

[50] Olga Khazan, "The More Gender Equality, the Fewer Women in STEM," The Atlantic (February 18, 2018). https://www.theatlantic.com/science/archive/2018/02/the-more-gender-equality-the-fewer- women-in-stem/553592/

[51] Mark J. Perry, "'Gender Gap in STEM'? Women are Majority of STEM Grad Students and they Earn a Majority of STEM Bachelor's Degrees," American Enterprise Institute (November 26, 2018). http://www.aei.org/publication/gender-gap-in-stem-women-are-majority-of-stem-grad-students- and-they-earn-a-majority-of-stem-bachelors-degrees/

[52] Khazan, "The More Gender Equality, the Fewer Women in STEM."

INDEX

INDEX

AUTHOR'S BIOGRAPHY AND CREDITS

ABOUT THE AUTHOR

After working for twenty years as a computer analyst, Mark R. Whittington became a freelance writer. He has worked for Yahoo News and currently writes regularly for The Hill and the Daily Caller on public policy aspects of space exploration. He has been published in the *Wall Street Journal, Forbes, Business Insider, USA Today*, and the *Washington Post*, among other venues.

PICTURE CREDITS

Everett Historical: 9, 12, 17; Library of Congress: 18, 21, 22; National Aeronautics and Space Administration: 85, 89, 93, 96; Used under license from Shutterstock, Inc.: 2, 26, 37, 41, 43, 49, 75, 76, 82, 90, 95; Benjamin Clapp / Shutterstock.com: 61; Rob Crandall / Shutterstock.com: 52; Diego G Diaz / Shutterstock.com: 24; Stephanie Kenner / Shutterstock.com: 15; Maverick Pictures / Shutterstock.com: 13; Jess Pomponio / Shutterstock.com: 1, 6; Lev Radin / Shutterstock.com: 53; Rblfmr / Shutterstock.com: 31; Mark Reinstein / Shutterstock.com: 60, 71; Rena Schild / Shutterstock.com: 64, 69, 79; Roger Sheldon / Shutterstock.com: 32; Karl Sonnenberg / Shutterstock.com: 57; Sundry Photography / Shutterstock.com: 46; US Navy Photo: 86; official White House Photo by Chuck Kennedy: 35.